THE SECRET HISTORY OF NEW JERSEY

Tony Gruenewald was born in Manhattan, but has lived most of his life in Edison, New Jersey. He has worked on a loading dock, as a fast food fish fryer and in radio journalism, advertising and the nonprofit world. To find out more and to stay up-to-date, visit him at **www.tonygruenewald.com**. Photo by John Larkin

Emily,
I think the Jacksons are going to
contact you about organizing up the
next Michael tribute. Thanks for
making my 50th
anniversary
a
memorable
one.
Tony

THE SECRET

HISTORY

OF NEW JERSEY

Poems by
Tony Gruenewald

Northwind Publishing

Published by Northwind Publishing
PO Box 823
Red Bank, N.J. 07701

Cover design, graphics and photos by Tony Gruenewald.
Author photo by John Larkin.

ISBN-13: 978-1-880764-25-1
ISBN-10: 1-880764-25-3

Published in 2009.
Printed by CreateSpace in the United States of America.

For Amanda, my love and my muse from whom I've stolen most of my best ideas.

Poets are from everywhere I guess…even from Edison.
Overheard at the Celebration of
New Jersey's Literary Journals

Contents

Exit 1–The Secret History of New Jersey

Exit 2–New York City, Boca Raton, Bluefield, W.Va., Afghanistan

EXIT 1

THE SECRET HISTORY OF NEW JERSEY

Next Right

Grand Finale

(Fourth of July, South Edison, New Jersey, early '70s)

Lit the last day of school,
the fuse slowly burned
to a crescendo.
Cherry bombs and M-80s
buzzed back yards
til a neighbor's shed, roof
or line of laundry
set ablaze exploded
into fire trucks, fist fights
and cops retreating,
chased by barrages of bottle rockets
through gunpowder fogged moonlight.

First Class

for Jerry Monastersky

My mother read between the mimeographed lines
of the letter sent home my first day of school;

though expectations were low,
they'd teach enough to know

how to sign away my soul
to the used car and mortgage,

and to please remember that I'd been bred
to be fed to the factories

and maybe marry the girl I met
behind the luncheonette counter after class.

I'd been blessed as nothing less than
assembly line fodder for Westinghouse, Revlon or Ford,

and that she would be grateful to them should they graduate me
to any institution more prestigious than

Rahway State
Prison.

Slow Children At Play

I wonder how they feel
those children who come home to find
a sign that says
Slow Children At Play
sprouted in front of their house.

I grew up in a time before
self-esteem,
before every Little League kid
was trophied just for showing up
and know my arch-nemesis
of a junior high gym teacher
would have gleefully planted such a sign
in front of my house
to further mock my
hormone-ravaged coordination.

He would have unveiled a sign
in front of the homes of each of my fellow
"Slow Boy Relay Team" members,
holding press conferences to recount with relish
a litany of incidents demonstrating
our appalling lack of athleticism.

And had we slow boys had access to such signs,
each of us, clinging desperately
to our lower rungs
on the adolescent ladder of brutality
would have planted them
up and down Crescent Road,
which for whatever reason

seemed to have more than its share of
a different kind of
Slow Children At Play.

My Scents of The Sixties

(Sorry Sam, I was too young for tear gas)

1.
Spring came with
the stale stick
of Topps bubble gum
perfuming
the sugar powder-pocked back
of my Gates Brown
baseball card.

2.
Morning meant
the sweet scent
of cinnamon raisin toast
while awaiting
a southerly breeze
to roll back
the refineries'
sulfury blanket.

3.
We swam through
summer afternoons
with the sharp shock
of chlorine
cutting through waves
of sultry steam
wafting from
block after block
of freshly rolled
asphalt.

4.
On summer evenings
we watched the cool kids
parade their stingray bikes
behind the pied piper
mosquito truck,
their procession weaving
in and out of
a DDT-laced shroud.

Ford Motor Company Edison Assembly Plant, 1948-2004

Suburbs sprouted
from surrounding fields
feeding it the sweat and muscle
that conceived
Jimmy Dean's and Steve McQueen's
silver screen
dream machines
on the midnight shift
to a turbocharged
tomorrow,
producing paychecks
for first roofs
not rented
and delivering
horsepower
to devour
the endless asphalt
toward a newly minted
American mirage.

Requiem for The Turnpike Drive-in
(About Those Ghosts in Your New House...)

I saw *Jaws* from your half bath while
perched atop the trunk of a sixty-eight
Impala convertible during a double feature
with some Vincent Price-Poe adaptation.

Soon you'll swim
in the refreshment stand
where we bought our popcorn
and Cokes and

we're all quite convinced that
the new Stop & Shop's produce manager
was conceived in your bedroom

in the back of his grandma's
borrowed station wagon.

Red Light District

Spring brings
road crews
sprouting like dandelions
destined to entomb me
in traffic
and fill my senses
with the scent of
out-of-tune diesel
inducing me to dream
of red lights
and scream
as I discover
I can determine
the make and model
of every vehicle
deemed deserving of fossil fuel
during the last four decades
from the size and shape
of its tail lights
and I swear
that the arrow on the sign
that leads to the on-ramp
is the tip of the tail
of the devil
himself
disguised in an orange safety vest
waving me through waves
of virgin asphalt steam
traffic flag in one hand
pitch fork in the other

Route 1 Free Association
(To the guy in the black Lincoln riding my bumper…)

You'd think you were Neal Cassady
if you only knew who he was,
but you don't,
so you also don't know
you're just settling
for fancying yourself a
James Dean, who unlike Cassady
couldn't handle the speed.

Cassady himself misunderstood,
but at least appreciated,
be bop,
which, some would say,
puts him one step ahead of me
and, I'd like to presume,
you.

But Dizzy Gillespie told Miles Davis,
that he, Davis,
didn't really get it either,
so once again,
Cassady was in
good company.

The mistake Cassady
and his beat boys made
was thinking those bop cats
hadn't planned
where they'd land
while they scaled
their musical slaloms,

which means
it would have had
everything in common
with this poem
if they were right,
which of course,
they weren't.

Personally, I prefer blues,
barbed wire raw,
as if the closest I'd been
to a plantation
wasn't the closely supervised
feeding, weeding and grooming
of my grandfather's ridiculously
green front lawn.

And, speaking of blues
and greens, that traffic light
just turned from green
to yellow and I pray
you're about to react
to my brake lights'
alarming red or
we'll both be singing
some serious
blues.

Proverbs I-95
(after Proverbs 6:16)

There are six things
the Lord hates,

yes, seven are an
abomination to Him;

tailgaters, lane weavers,
those who eschew
turn signals or get into the wrong
toll lane, those who proceed too
slowly in passing lanes, or merge
unsafely, these are

forgiven by the Lord.
And this is yet another
reason you should be

thankful since He is obviously
much more tolerant of
your driving
than I.

The Migration of the Butterfly Tattoo

A butterfly flashed
past my windshield
at seventy miles per hour
emerging from the chrysalis
of a pair of low-rider jeans,
its wings revealed from beneath
a billowing cropped t-shirt
while clinging for life
on the back of a Harley
swerving serpentine
around the rush hour
semis, SUVs and sedans
riding the jetstream
of U.S. 1 and disappearing
until I saw it again
a half hour down the road,
perched in the parking lot
of the Bennigan's
on the clover leaf
to Route 18.

A Study of the Social Order of Automobiles

When your Subaru left the inspection station
like Hester Prynne,
its scarlet rejection sticker conspicuous,
the other cars did not shun it,
it was their drivers whose eyes
were either averted
or overflown with disdain.

You'll never see
a Lamborghini or Porsche
roll their headlights
in disgust
when parked
next to a Kia.

And the BMWs did not
call the authorities
when I drove my Hyundai
though their neighborhood,
having us pulled over and questioned,
suspicious of the aliens in their midst,
their officer explaining,
people from here don't drive those.

Suspicious Skin

1.
My former girlfriend's family joked
that her baby brother
with his Catalan complexion
and dark crown of curls
resembled every terror suspect
whose mug made
the evening news.

2.
Ever since September Eleventh
every entrepreneur
of suspicious skin
assures his security
by wrapping his establishment
in Old Glory
and neon declarations
of God Bless America.

3.
When I reported black ice
the receptionist
scrambled building security
to protect against
black guys
in the parking lot.

Bound Brook Train Station

Like bare branched trees
skewering fire seared soil
antenna limbs shiver naked
atop abandoned brownstones
planted along apathy scorched asphalt,

scratching at skies
saturated with electronic signals
and sunlight
that no longer
spark any of them
to life.

Shipwrecked

The sun melted into the Caribbean
like orange and lemon sherbet
onto a rippling blue bowl

She leaned against the ship's railing
as we satiated ourselves
on the sumptuous tropical sunset

She said it reminded her of sunsets
on Lake Something-or-another
at home in Vermont

I recalled the setting sun
reflecting off the refinery towers
along the Jersey Turnpike

She said nothing
leaving to find someone
who shared her subjective sense of romance

Late Again Cantata
(NJ Transit, Conductor)

Commuters groan on cell phones
rhapsodizing to the rhythm
of fingers tapping
their touch tone timpani
when the conductor instructs
we're stuck in the swamps of Secaucus
playin' them waitin' on another
Amtrak to pass again blues.

Playin' Them Penn Station Rush Hour Musical Chairs Blues

Anxiously they wait
Reflexes peaked
Concentration complete

The air,
thick with
anticipation
is cut
by the flicking
departure board
unleashing
this human
tsunami

As if the ensuing
announcement
was for videos
of J-Lo's
sex life, Giuliani
bobbleheads
or some other
bauble of
a fallen humanity
and not

The New Jersey Transit Trenton local is now receiving
*   passengers*
on track number four.

Fetch

Like retrievers,
our eyes fixed on
our master's every twitch,
the departure board
sends us springing–
a single-purposed hurry
bounding in pursuit of
our just flushed quarry–
the 7:02 Trenton Express
now boarding
on track number twelve.

Highlights from the Permanent Collection

Lifting your head from your paperback distraction
you spy the horizon from the seclusion of
your elsewhere-bound express and think
you're traveling through the country's alimentary canal,
a state that's home to everything
you'd never wish
on anyone's back yard.

But upon closer inspection you'd find
you're now contemplating Mondrian's
"A Composition in Shipping Containers."
from the New Jersey Transit
Ride-Through Museum of Art's
permanent collection.

See the Skyway hopscotching its way
across the remarkably unmysterious marsh?
It's the focal point of the classic
"Twilight on the Swamp"
from that oft-overlooked
Passaic River School of painters.

And that graffiti-tattooed abandoned factory
is the controversial Hopper-Basquiat mash-up
you'd have read about
had you not been off
on your quaint little trip
to The Louvre.

The rest of your novel can wait
while you savor
the Turnpike, the tank farms,
the tattered trestles
and all the other masterpieces
carefully curated like the flavors
of a feast for your eyes.

Bon appetit!

Directions

I live a few minutes from Exit 10
of the Jersey Turnpike
where a dozen highways knot
like a bowl of asphalt sauced
spaghetti
then spew you out
in a dozen different directions,
rarely the one you've intended,
since the road signs
mean what they say
but hardly ever say what they
mean
and some of our streets
are known by at least three names,
while the same name is claimed
by several very different roads,
with at least one being
a place you'd never ever want to stop
unless your sole source of income
or fun
involves things that interest mainly
undercover cops.

So here's what cha do:
once you pay the toll,
bear right and exit left
on the split to 440 South
which becomes 287 North
where you exit for Route 1 South
via 531 South,
which is also known as Main Street,
and is not to be confused

with 514 East,
which you have to pass
as it becomes
another Main Street…

Better yet,
get off at Exit 9.
It's a little out of the way,
but a missed turn
can't land you
on the Outerbridge
to Staten Island.

The Last Temptation of Cracker Jack Christ

The college kid hawking Cracker Jacks
at Commerce Bank Ballpark looks down,
and in surfer dude drawl
calls across the vast lawn seat chaos,

Ma'am your son just stole your purse,
her four year old towing
her battle ship of a shoulder bag
dredging up grass,
in steadfast pursuit
of his messiah
of sweets salvation.

The boy stops,
drives his hands
into the bag's massive maw,
then raises them up
as if in worship
of his Cracker Jack Christ,

fists full of dollars
offered as gladly as first fruits
to the lord of all things
gooey and sticky and sweet.

Cracker Jack calls again,
Ma'am, he's trying to hand me money
and I'm tempted to take it,

then takes a deep breath
and pulls back his hands saying,

I can't do this, I can't do this,
and retreats across the lawn
toward the relative order
of the not-quite-so-cheap seats

leaving once-twined teenagers
and wrestling children
parted in his wake.

New Jersey's Problem Poets

New Jersey Walks a Tightrope In Handling Its Poet Problem
– *The New York Times* June 28, 2003

The only way to deal with the deer problem is to reduce the size of the herd. – Tom Poole, Chairman, Princeton Deer Problem Evaluation Committee.

The theory goes: The aroma of
coffee brewing in big box book stores
attracted them; those who'd
thought Walt Whitman a bridge and
never knew the distinction of
simile and metaphor were
exposed to the virus, propagating till
all considered themselves poets.

At first it was considered commendable,
poetry's contemplation flowering
from the cracks of an instant access culture.
Migrating from venue to venue,
they swarmed the lists of
local open mikes, spreading
epidemics of raggedy
rhythm and messy meter.

Soon enough, the once few
who'd kept the candle so hidden that
the flame'd been considered
eternally doused wondered,
*What to do about those
faulty footed free-versers
and rough rhyming rappers*

waxing universal,
overrunning our neatly
enjambed, self-referential
stanzas?

What to do?

What to do?

Pilgrimage

for Judy Wilson-Smith

If the world wasn't round
they'd have journeyed
from its four corners to
their Jersey Jerusalem
their Mercer Street Mecca
their Princeton Promised Land
their Garden State Graceland.

And though the long-late great man
hasn't retrieved a letter
in their lifetime
these pilgrims tiptoe giddily
to his once-upon-a-time front porch

to smile while comforted by
the camera's confirming click
that captures their fulfillment
finally complete, found in
fondling Einstein's mailbox.

Dr. Strangelawn
(or Why I Learned To Loathe My Lawn)

My neighbors arm for chemical warfare.
Their windchimes ring in a new spring:
time to deploy their weapons of mass destruction
determined to drive the demon dandelion from
the politically determined sovereignty of
Kentucky Blue and Rye.

Why?,
I ask rhetorically
since my neighbors are entranced
in crusade-like zeal
to recreate nature in the image of
some revisionist natural history.

Who decided the dandelion was evil?
When did this happen,
and why?
Did they, the dandelions, participate
in the debate?
or were they excluded

their lobby shut out, left powerless
by lawn pharmacists
profit driven to pump the ground full of
lab concocted cocktails?

Herbicidal maniacs
deciding which species should be celebrated,
and which ones
scorned,
in the name of creating
a chemically dependent
suburban master race;

a proud parade of green and preened
pedigreed properties on display.
But to their dismay,
summer brings
drought
leaving drug-induced dreamlawns
unable to cope
when exposed to the harsh sunlight
of reality;

left to go
cold turkey,
block after block of well bred Kentucky Blue blades,
whither, pathetically begging
for a fix or at least admission
to a Betty Ford Clinic
for chemically dependent lawns,
while the weeds, thru sheer stubborn
determination and
natural selection
survive the onslaught in spring,
and flourish, smugly singing
in Dylanesque whine

How does it feel?

From the Memoir of The Minister of Propaganda

I stayed
only because every day
promised to be
more absurd
than the last,
and the day before
was always
more absurd
than the day before it,
especially after the CEO
told his toadies
to buy up every bolt
of camouflage material
in the state
and turn it into
tablecloths for the boardroom,
pennants hung from every few feet
of ceiling grid
and a sign that filled the wall
behind the receptionist's desk in the lobby
blaring out in felt block letters:
WE'RE AT WAR …AND WE'RE GOING TO WIN!

He renamed the cafeteria the mess hall,
the boardroom the war room,
the lavatories latrines and
had my boss have me,
as much a master wordworker
as they could afford,
create military sounding slogans
to be cast on camouflage

and hung throughout our corporate headquarters
turned executive asylum.

So, I followed his example,
retitled myself
Minister of Propaganda
and listened in as he attempted
to requisition a decommissioned tank
from the local Army Reserve base .

And as camouflage was designed to do,
it pretty quickly blended into the corporate grey walls
and the hemorrhaging red ink,
unless I looked in the eyes
of a visiting vendor who was expecting
business as usual,
or later, for the easily duped,
payment upon completion of said business.

Like I said,
I stuck around only because
every day promised
to be more absurd than the last,
which surely took a lot of talent
and even greater imagination,
all of which kept me
endlessly entertained,
because as I told the disbelieving civilians
back home,
not even I
could make this stuff up,
and carried on carefree until
the guy who supplied our sanitation services
told one of the bosses that

he knew how to stuff the boss's body
into one of his unpaid for dumpsters
in such a way that
it would never ever be found and…
oh yeah…the bosses said
they couldn't afford to pay for me anymore, either.

The Secret History of New Jersey

It is believed by some
that the apostle Paul
sowed the seeds
of the first
jug handle
when he wrote
in his much disputed
and in some traffic circles
deeply discredited
second epistle
to the Colonians that
all turns,
even those to the left
should indeed begin
from the lane of right.

This was written
during the brief reign
of the vastly underappreciated
Emperor Secaucus,
who passed through
the town now bearing his name
to review his troops
when the Roman Empire
sprawled its most westward
after conquering the last
Greek diner
located on
the outskirts
of Sparta.

After that, history unfurled
pretty much as reported
except that
nearly a millenium
after Paul's letter
to the Leonians
Vikings started
to settle
Cranfjord,
while to the south
Vandalized villagers
commemorated their plight by
building a bridge proclaiming:

Trenton Makes The World Takes.

EXIT 2

New York City
Boca Raton
Bluefield W Va
Afghanistan

Next Right

The Venn of Everything

*The Venn Diagram is made up of two or more overlapping circles.
It is often used in mathematics to show relationships between sets.
In language arts instruction, Venn Diagrams are useful for
examining similarities and differences in characters, stories,
poems, etc.*

Long after we overhear
the couple at the next table
tell their friends about finding
the gay-friendly synagogue
they call Shabbat Shebang

we pay our bill and spill
into the ever-swirling
Venn kaleidoscope
of Washington Square;

each of us parts of sets
whirling into alignment
with sets with which
we'd never imagine communion

while putting people into focus
with whom we'd never dreamed
we'd ever share
a common ground.

The Summer After...

Though from New Jersey,
I become the local color,
naming mysterious
landmasses, bridges
and buildings
from atop the Empire State Building,
a quizzical
Babel awash in
foreign tongues and
native accents.

But only when looking
south does anyone
hand me their camera,
filling photo albums
around the world
with couples, backs to
the southwest, their
smiling faces supplanting
the aching abyss
in the skyline.

Curt Flood

I'm pleased God made my skin black. I wish He had made it thicker.   Curt Flood

It wasn't
just the nightly torrent of taunts
from fans and teammates alike,
or the Jim Crow restrooms,
restaurants and motels during
the long rickety Southern League bus rides
that finally broke the 19 year old rookie from
the slums of Oakland in '57.

It was between games of a doubleheader;
everyone stripped their sweaty, dusty flannels
and left them in a pile
to be quickly laundered
for the nightcap.

He watched the clubhouse attendant approach
the pile with a long stick,
fishing his uniform away
from his teammates' and
at arms length
carry it to
the *Colored Only* cleaners
across town.

While his teammates took the field
in their freshly laundered flannels,
he sat alone,
naked.

Leaving A Lasting Impression

He mutters,
Oooh baby,
you're so sweeeet,
just loud enough
for her to hear
from the doorway
of an 8th Street bodega
his words an itching,
twitching switchblade
scratching sharply
at her psyche.

Then he blows a kiss.
It hits her
like a blackjacked
fist.

Tony the Fool

*One of the faults we have with Jews is this: you are a very
minuscule part of the population of America, but a very major part
of the influence. What made you do that?... What do you know that
makes you the powerful, influential, and well-living people that
you are?* Louis Farrakhan

I feel the scribes' eyes study
as they scribble on napkins
and notepads from the
tables of kosher pizzerias.
They input into palm pilots
and laptops on trains and
planes faithfully documenting
for future generations
as they await the coming
(or coming again)
when their notes will be
transcribed into the
chapters and verses telling
the humbling tale of
Tony the Fool; the antithesis
of Solomon and his supposed
wisdom; destined to be the butt
of an eternity of jokes;
the Jew not attuned
to the plan, oblivious to
the spoils so
obviously his.

I avail myself of
all means of modern
communication: e-mail,

voice mail and satellite,
and search the faces of
strangers and
acquaintances for
signals more subtle:
a wink, a nod or secret
handshake of
notice of when and where
my fellow Jews congregate to conspire
for continued control
of culture
and commerce.
So, to you Reverend Farrakhan,
Tiny Tim McVeigh and all
the other brothers and sisters
under the hood,
thank you, for exposing
this unobservant Jew
as a fool
of biblical
proportion.

Comfort Food (1/1/02)

If all the cows, chickens and
other assorted animals
served tonight
on platters and buns
in the bars and bistros
of this stretch of Florida highway
congad to the slaughterhouse,
the parade might
circle the earth,
stretch to Mars
and back to this strip mall's
faux Chinese chain restaurant
across from the airport,
googleplex cinema
and university
in Boca Raton.

No one eats home here.
Every restaurant requires a wait
and on this unremarkable night
some nation's GNP
will be equalled
in tips alone.

And here at PF Chang's,
while the beach blonde waitress
promptly serves portions
confirming any
obesity study,
no one pays
attention as

the soundless TV
above the bar
serves up
censor-approved sights of

food
bombs dropping on
Afghanistan.

Love, American Style

In God We Trust
has been enshrined
on nickels and dollars and dimes
since His only Son
was crucified and died
on the dollar sign

The Almighty

sacrificed
to boost
our bottom line

Our Savior
risen indeed

Foregone

From a highway
cut like a ledge
in the mountain
we descend
through clouds
of foliage until
we see white steeples
and the promise of
the old coal town
of her youth
below.

We land on
a faded movie set
of a down town,
where even the graffiti
is beaten of bravado
and the gauntlet of
Norman Rockwell storefronts,
empty as the milk carton
skittering along the gutter are

FOR SALE…FOR RENT…FORECLOSED…FOREVER

impenetrable godwit bloodbath

subject line of an e-mail spam

What could this be, sent by
the mythical LaDonna Ott,
obviously an alias for a
counter terrorism super agent?

A warning about a fundamentalist
organization beyond the knowledge
of Homeland Security or even Fox News,
training in Starbuckistan or some other
former Soviet state desperate for some
world stage attention, its baristas
infiltrating, sneaking caffeinated
contraband past baggage check

to loose lethal intifada into
the lattes of Los Angeles,
Las Vegas, the Louvre or some
other L-place the codebreakers and
translators haven't quite been able to
confirm?

Vulnerable

I'd not noticed
the word had gone on vacation,
slipping off unannounced
to some uncharted precinct
of my brain with which
I'm not at all acquainted.

I'd not noticed
it was away until
involved in a conversation
which could not continue
without its participation.

A few hours later,
after a cheap flight back
from the Isle of Aphasia,
it unpacked its overnight bag
and asked,
Did you miss me?

Junky

for Bernadette, who once told me, straight faced, that she was down to
eighteen cups a day

To decaf
or not to decaf
that
is the question
whether tis nobler
in the mind
to suffer the slings and arrows
of outrageous headache
from
cold turkey caffeine withdrawal
or succumb
to the sweet siren scent
of another cup

I am a poet
or, so they sometimes tell me
and have grown accustomed to
working for beans
from Columbia or Kenya
ground and brewed
to speed through my impatient veins

lab coated clinicians tell me
it's only a caffeine delivery system
but how does that help me
when there's a Starbucks
on every corner
desperate to feed my desperate hunger
and I sometimes slip into a humbled mantra of

Our Father who art in
Columbia
and look for proof that
Juan Valdez
is not a mere myth of marketing
or the cause of my descent,
but the second coming
heaven sent
to search hill and valley
for that heavenly scent
of perfect blend of beans
for the faithful
Oh diner waitress
angel of mercy
fifteen percent
is not enough
to express appreciation
for your bottomless
second cup
For my name is Tony G.
and I am
a coffeeholic

A Poem For Plumbers

I am impotent
lost in the labyrinth
of plumbing that plagues
my existence. Pipe wrenches,
washers, teflon tape,
all rendered useless,
their inventions voided
by my uncouth hands.

For the god of domesticated
water mocks me or at best
does not consider my
petitions and prayers: valves forever
frozen open or shut, whichever
is least desirable, threads eternally
crossed or stripped, faucet leaks
reverberating like 3 a.m. thunder.

Ecstasy is:
the number of an honest
plumber; one whose sympathetic
touch can sooth the savage
sweat of my sickly
pipes and spigots
and whose smile
won't seem patronizing
after reviewing the results
of my humiliating attempts
to perform an act
of plumbing.

Why Do You Think They Call It Clicking A Mouse?

The computer geeks lie
and try to tell me that
by pecking these keys

I unleash streams of
zeros and ones which
arrange themselves as

letters and words on my monitor.
But I know the truth:
the glass masks teams of

hamsters tirelessly turning letters in time
to my rhythm less keystrokes
bustling like a crew of

caffeine and benzedrine steamed
Vanna Whites, each letter later traveling by
messenger amoeba to the bespectacled

ink-stain-apronned descendants
of Gutenberg's mice that call
my printer their home.

From *Snoopy: The Red Baron Years...*

Why the World War I Flying Ace?
Just a diversion to keep my mind
from what Sparky never knew:
all I wanted to do every time
the Bumstead's dog Daisy
was in heat was to break out,
that her scent wafted across the pencil thin pen
he put around our strip, forcing me to fantasize
about the French Foreign Legion and Sopwith Camels
or else go mad from desire.

And the old man must have been deaf
not to hear the ruckus going on
in the inky suburbs surrounding ours:
Chip's music from the Flagston's
keeping us up all night,
Sargeant Snorkel's daily thrashing of Beetle
echoing off the walls of Camp Swampy,
and just last night I woke up panting,
ran into the house
and curled up next to the Round Headed Kid,
the anger of the Mitchell's
What to do about Dennis arguments
still fracturing my dreams.

Vacancy

They're the failing letters
of the dull neon sign
outside the motel
on the state road
that lost relevance
when the interstate
pushed through
a few years back,
taking traffic
a couple miles west
with it
and sprouting
a Motel 6,
Econolodge
and casino
by its banks.

The pool's been filled in
and the road
doesn't even rate
a scenic route
on the way
to grandma's anymore.

Even the gas station's
pulled up pumps,
reinventing itself
a One Stop Travel Shop
with six packs, Subway and
Krispy Kremes delivered daily,
next to the Cracker Barrel,

next to the Days Inn,
that's next to
their freshly etched
six-lane
river of life.

Minivanned families
who,
after getting gas,
miss the interstate's entrance
and find this
the first late night light
won't dare to stop.
They flee,
spitting up
the parking lot's gravel of
busted gin bottles,
cigarette butts,
crushed beer cans and
spent condoms,
though the theme park's still
a good day's drive,
the kids are cranky
and dad's eyelids
are way past
half mast.

They can hear
the spasms of the N
and the top half of the second
C of the VACANCY sign's
intermittent buzz
against the distant traffic's roar

as they vainly try to light,
occasionally flaring disturbingly,
like my thoughts,
before the first good jolt
of caffeine
kicks in.

Steel Belted Lullaby

This midnight, I hear the highway crash
and recede like waves
within earshot of my bedroom window.

I yearn to grab my keys and hear
my engine hum–
part of the Great Gear Shifter's Symphony
playing on backroads and interstates,
in the big city's asphalt canyons
and along desolate desert two-lanes.

Seeing the highway roll out before me–
an infinite red carpet inviting me on
in my throne of
internal combustion.

Hearing steel belts sing
like a bow against strings
of interstate asphalt.

Reading billboards like haiku,
mile markers as history,
and traffic signs my gospel:
Thou shalt not exceed 65,
while crossing the hairs of
radar guns; tempting troopers
lurking like gators in the grass,
only their bubble gum machine lights
visible above the median grade.

Hearing diesels idle
chattering like crickets
in the hazy rest stop night
their downshifts
true American arias
serenading me to sleep
through cheap motel walls.

Sashaying down
small town boulevards
leaving trails of bassline thunder
deep dark delta blues
reverberating in my wake.
Closing my eyes at night and seeing
the last several hundred miles of
white lines reflash faster
than the law allows.

Burning like Sherman through the soul of Dixie
passing pickup trucks sporting shot gun racks,
NASCAR stickers and confederate flags

A highway cowboy,
my Chisholm Trail skid-mark scarred
and littered with remains
of retread tires.

Spitting gravel and
disappearing
down some old dirt road
taillights like tracers
through clouds of dust at dusk.

In The Still Of The Night

It's always after midnight
or 11 o'clock
at the earliest
since Sunday morning
is the only other time
conditions support
such harmonies
and this is not
a Sunday morning
kind of song

From the control room
the engineer peers
through stagnant
cigarette smoke
indifferent to
another five kids
surrounding the mic
they hope
holds magic

White shirt sleeves
rolled to the elbow
exposing raw boned hunger
practicing one last time
what they'd sung on
street corners and stairways
like the group
the night before
or the night before that...
their lives teetering
on every note

AM Radio

Radio is a sound salvation. Elvis Costello

When Sunset waves her wondrous wand
sending radio signals reeling off the heavens
she grants me
baseball from Atlanta,
interstate traffic for truckers and
country music for all from the Carolinas.

So even as a child
empowered by only a few
transistors, two double-As
and an AM dial I had
French Canadian rock & roll…
Detroit…St. Louis…Cleveland…
half a continent
controlled by a fingertip.

Star light, star bright
first star I see tonight
winking red atop a transmitter tower,
flirting with the infinite night;
even now, as I hustle down
Florida's endless peninsula,
you soothe me with a familiar lullaby
of *LIE, GWB*
and the Turnpike's northern terminus
on traffic reports from home
near NYC.

Notes

Ford Motor Company Edison Assembly Plant, 1948-2004
The workers at this plant built the 1948 Mercury, the car made famous by James Dean in *Rebel Without A Cause*, and the early model Mustangs. Steve McQueen drove one of these in the film *Bullitt*, which featured a groundbreaking chase scene through the streets of San Francisco. It closed in 2004, was leveled and is being redeveloped as Edison Towne Center.

New Jersey's Problem Poets
During the 2002 Geraldine R. Dodge Poetry Festival at Waterloo Village in New Jersey, then state poet laureate Amiri Baraka read a piece call "Somebody Blew Up America" which included the assertion that the Israeli government knew that the attacks on the World Trade Center on September 11, 2001 were going to happen and allowed them to be carried out. Let's just say that people were not happy with Mr. Baraka. Within a week there were moves in the state legislature to have him removed from office. There was one problem–the bill that created the position had no provision to fire the poet laureate. Nearly a year later, at the end of the legislative session, the lawmakers voted to eliminate the position. In the weeks leading up to that decision, *The New York Times* ran an article with the headline, "New Jersey Walks a Tightrope In Handling Its Poet Problem."

At the same time, the Princeton area had a problem with its deer population. Much of the rest of the state has the same issue. Suburban sprawl has encroached on the wooded areas where deer and other wildlife have thrived. Solutions have ranged from controlled hunts to birth control.

The Secret History of New Jersey
Leonia, Colonia, Secaucus, Cranford and Sparta are towns in
New Jersey. One of the bridges that spans the Delaware River
from Trenton, the state capital and a once-thriving industrial
city, as neon lettering that reads *Trenton Makes The World
Takes*. Those who aren't familiar with New Jersey highways
panic when the try to make a left turn, because on many of
them you can't make a left turn from the left lane. You have to
exit the highway and make the left at the light at the end of a
jug handle.

From Snoopy: The Red Baron Years
Sparky was the nickname of Charles Schultz, the creator of
"Peanuts."

Acknowledgments

Grateful acknowledgment to the publications where some of
these peoms first appeared:
Edison Literary Review: "Ford Motor Company Edison
        Assembly Plant, 1948-2004", "Foregone", "My Scents
        of the Sixties", "AM Radio", "A Poem For Plumbers"
        and "Shipwrecked"
The New York Times: "Proverbs I-95"
Up and Under: "The Secret History of New Jersey"
FZQ: "Junky"
Exit 13: "Pilgrimage", "The Summer After…" and "Requiem
        for the Turnpike Drive-in"
U.S.1 Worksheets: "First Class"
U.S. 1: The Newspaper: "Grand Finale". "Dr. Strangelawn (or
        Why I Learned to Loathe My Lawn)", "Directions",
        "From the Memoir of the Minister of Propaganda",
        "Late Again Cantata", "Route 1 Free Association" and
        "Red Light District"

Identity Theory: "Vacancy"
The Idiom: "From: *Snoopy: The Red Baron Years*"
Slow Trains: "Curt Flood", "New Jersey's Problem Poets",
"impenetrable godwit bloodbath" and "Playin' Them
Penn Station Rush Hour Musical Chair Blues"
English Journal: "The Venn of Everything"
Sunken Lines: "Tony the Fool", "Why Do You Think They Call
It Clicking A Mouse?", "A Study of the Social Order
of Automobiles" and "Comfort Food (1/1/02)"

"Red Light District" and "Route 1 Free Association" also
appeared in *Slow Trains.*
"Dr. Strangelawn (or Why I Learned To Loathe My Lawn)"
also appeared in *Thatchwork*, an anthology from Delaware
Valley Poets.
"My Scents of the Sixties" also appeared in *Baby Boomer
Birthright*, an anthology by PoetWorks Press.

3172017

Made in the USA